BLUE WORLDS

THE ATLANTIC OCEAN

Anita Ganeri
Josy Bloggs

WAYLAND

First published in Great Britain in 2022
by Wayland

Copyright © Hodder and Stoughton 2022

All rights reserved

Editors: Julia Bird; Julia Adams
Design: Peter Clayman
Illustrations: Josy Bloggs

HB ISBN 978 1 5263 1562 5
PB ISBN 978 1 5263 1570 0

10 9 8 7 6 5 4 3 2 1

Wayland, an imprint of
Hachette Children's Group
Part of Hodder and Stoughton
Carmelite House
50 Victoria Embankment
London EC4Y 0DZ

An Hachette UK Company
www.hachette.co.uk
www.hachettechildrens.co.uk

Printed and bound in UAE

The website addresses (URLs) included in this book were valid at the time of going to press. However, it is possible that contents or addresses may have changed since the publication of this book. No responsibility for any such changes can be accepted by either the author or the Publisher.

Contents

The blue planet 4
Around the Atlantic 6
Beneath the waves 8
Volcanoes and islands 10
Winds, weather and currents 12
Exploring the Atlantic 14
Atlantic wildlife 16
The Sargasso Sea 18
Atlantic green turtles 20
People and transport 22
Riches of the Atlantic 24
Atlantic in danger 26
Future Atlantic 28
Atlantic facts 30
Glossary 31
Index 32

The blue planet

Earth has five oceans – the Atlantic, Pacific, Indian, Arctic and Southern Oceans. The Atlantic is our second largest ocean, stretching for thousands of kilometres north and south of the equator.

Changing oceans

Two hundred million years ago, there was one vast ocean, called Panthalassa, surrounding a giant landmass, called Pangaea. Pangaea gradually broke up into today's continents. Where the Americas, Europe and Africa pulled apart, the Atlantic Ocean was formed.

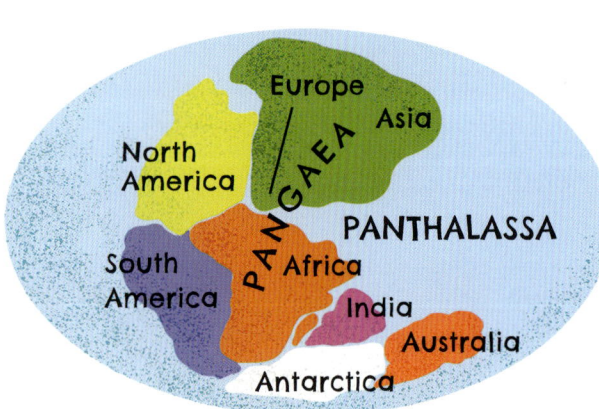

The Atlantic and us

Like the other oceans, the Atlantic is vitally important for life on Earth. Its water helps form part of the water cycle, its currents help spread heat around the Earth and it provides food and transport routes for millions of people.

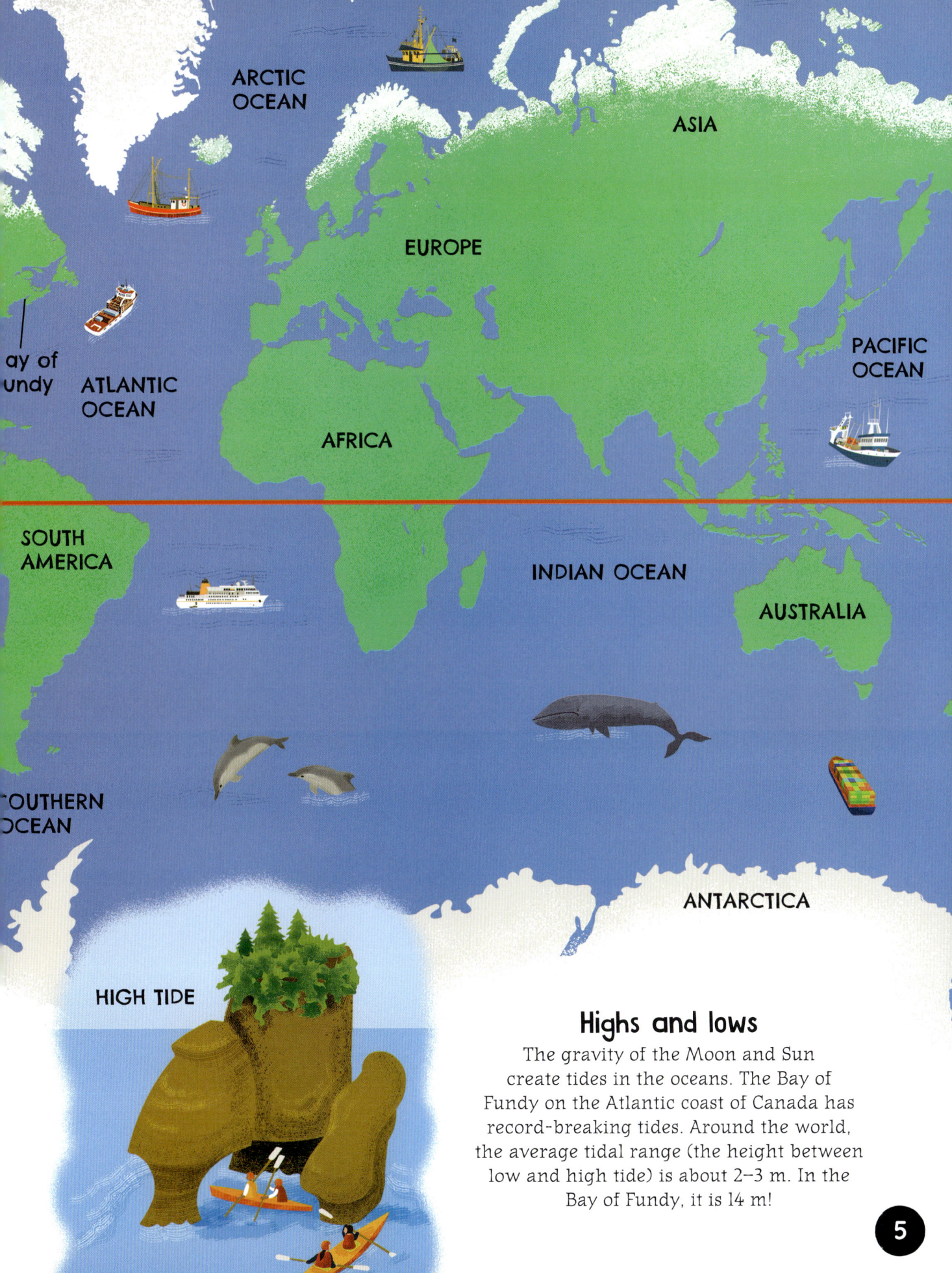

Highs and lows

The gravity of the Moon and Sun create tides in the oceans. The Bay of Fundy on the Atlantic coast of Canada has record-breaking tides. Around the world, the average tidal range (the height between low and high tide) is about 2–3 m. In the Bay of Fundy, it is 14 m!

Around the Atlantic

The Atlantic Ocean lies between the continents of North America and South America to the west, and Europe and Africa to the east. Its northern and southern parts connect to icy, polar oceans.

Atlantic rivers

Many of the world's great rivers drain their waters into the Atlantic Ocean. They include the Mississippi, the Amazon, the Congo and the Rhine. Sediment from the Amazon river forms a giant fan on the seabed of the Atlantic.

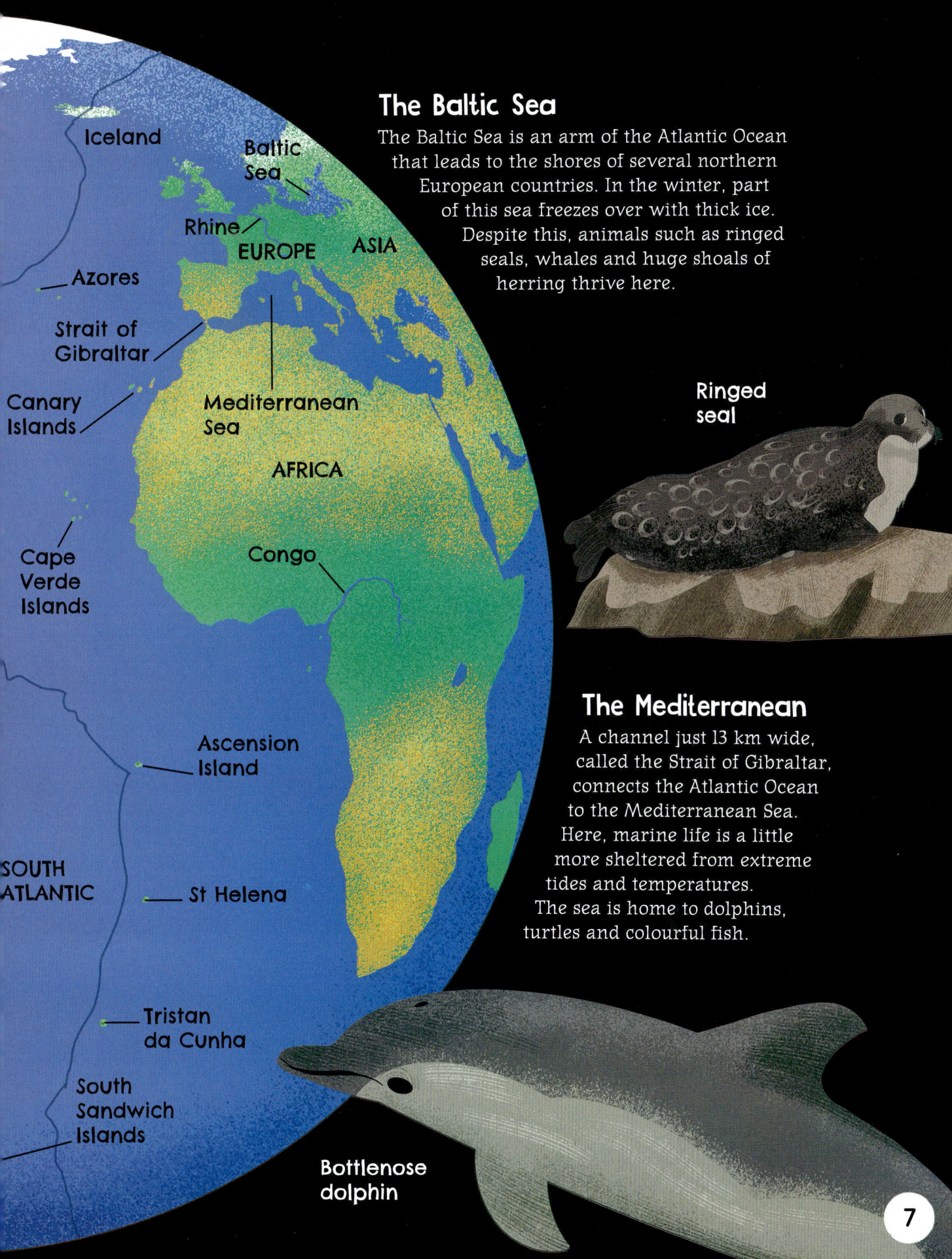

The Baltic Sea

The Baltic Sea is an arm of the Atlantic Ocean that leads to the shores of several northern European countries. In the winter, part of this sea freezes over with thick ice. Despite this, animals such as ringed seals, whales and huge shoals of herring thrive here.

The Mediterranean

A channel just 13 km wide, called the Strait of Gibraltar, connects the Atlantic Ocean to the Mediterranean Sea. Here, marine life is a little more sheltered from extreme tides and temperatures. The sea is home to dolphins, turtles and colourful fish.

Beneath the waves

The Earth's crust is divided into sections, called tectonic plates. Where the plates meet, they can change the landscape above them, creating mountains, or deep rifts. The Atlantic lies above the African, South American, Eurasian and North American tectonic plates.

Ocean trenches

In a subduction zone, one tectonic plate slides slowly under another. This creates a deep trench in the ocean floor. The deepest trench in the Atlantic is the Puerto Rico Trench which lies 8,605 m below the surface.

Central ridge

Running down the centre of the Atlantic is the 16,000-km Mid-Atlantic Ridge. This is a spreading ridge – a range of underwater mountains where tectonic plates are slowly moving apart. As the plates separate, hot rock called magma rises from under the crust, and cools to form new rock.

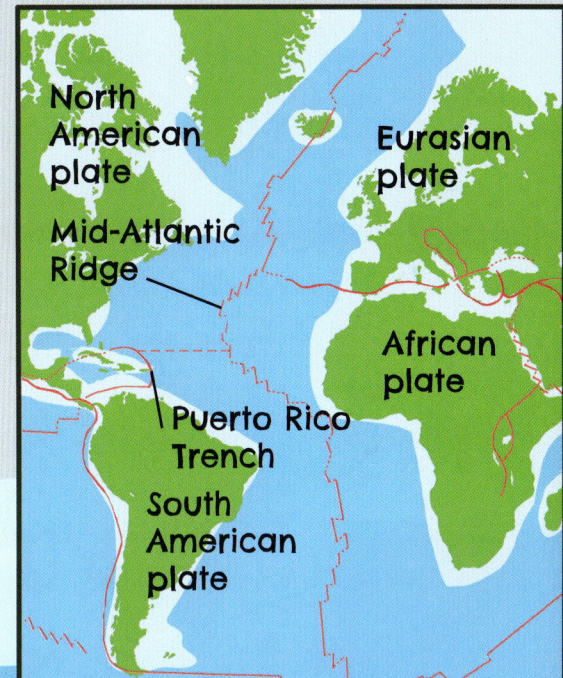

Underwater plains

On either side of the Mid-Atlantic Ridge, more than 4,000 m below the water's surface, lie vast flat areas called abyssal plains. Covered with deep layers of sediment, these are some of the flattest places on Earth.

Volcanoes and islands

Along the Mid-Atlantic Ridge, magma rises from beneath the Earth's crust to the surface to form volcanoes. Most of these volcanoes erupt deep under the waves, but some grow high enough to break the surface and form islands.

Iceland

The island of Iceland sits at the northern end of the Mid-Atlantic Ridge. The ridge runs right through the middle of the island, marked by a rocky gorge. As a result, Iceland has many active volcanoes, some hidden under ice caps.

Azores

The Azores lie where the Mid-Atlantic Ridge meets the boundary between the Eurasian plate and African plate. Each of the nine islands is the tip of a giant underwater volcano. Other remote, volcanic Atlantic islands include Ascension Island, St Helena and Tristan da Cunha.

Island arcs

Volcanoes often form close to undersea subduction zones. Magma rises on one side of the zone, creating a line of volcanic islands called an island arc. The South Sandwich Islands in the southern Atlantic, and the Lesser Antilles in the Caribbean Sea are all island arcs.

Winds, weather and currents

The waters of the Atlantic are always on the move. Currents carry warm or cold water around the ocean, driven by the wind. These currents affect the climate of the land they flow past and can cause extreme weather events.

Hurricanes

Destructive tropical storms called hurricanes form high above the Atlantic. They begin life as groups of powerful thunderstorms that then start spinning, gathering energy from the warm, tropical waters. When hurricanes meet land, they can destroy whole cities and cause huge floods.

Trades and westerlies

Atlantic wind patterns called trades and westerlies can influence the path of a hurricane. Trade winds form north and south of the equator; further north and south, westerlies blow in the opposite direction. As they form and gather speed, hurricanes often follow the paths of the trades and westerlies.

Atlantic gyres

Currents also often play a part in the formation of a hurricane. Gyres are circular currents north and south of the equator that are driven by winds. Thunderstorms often form above these currents and the winds that accompany them can sometimes develop into hurricanes.

The Gulf Stream

Flowing north from the Gulf of Mexico, the Gulf Stream carries warm water up the eastern coastline of North America, then across to Europe. This brings mild temperatures to the coasts of northern Europe. The warm water of the stream also helps hurricanes form and intensify along its path.

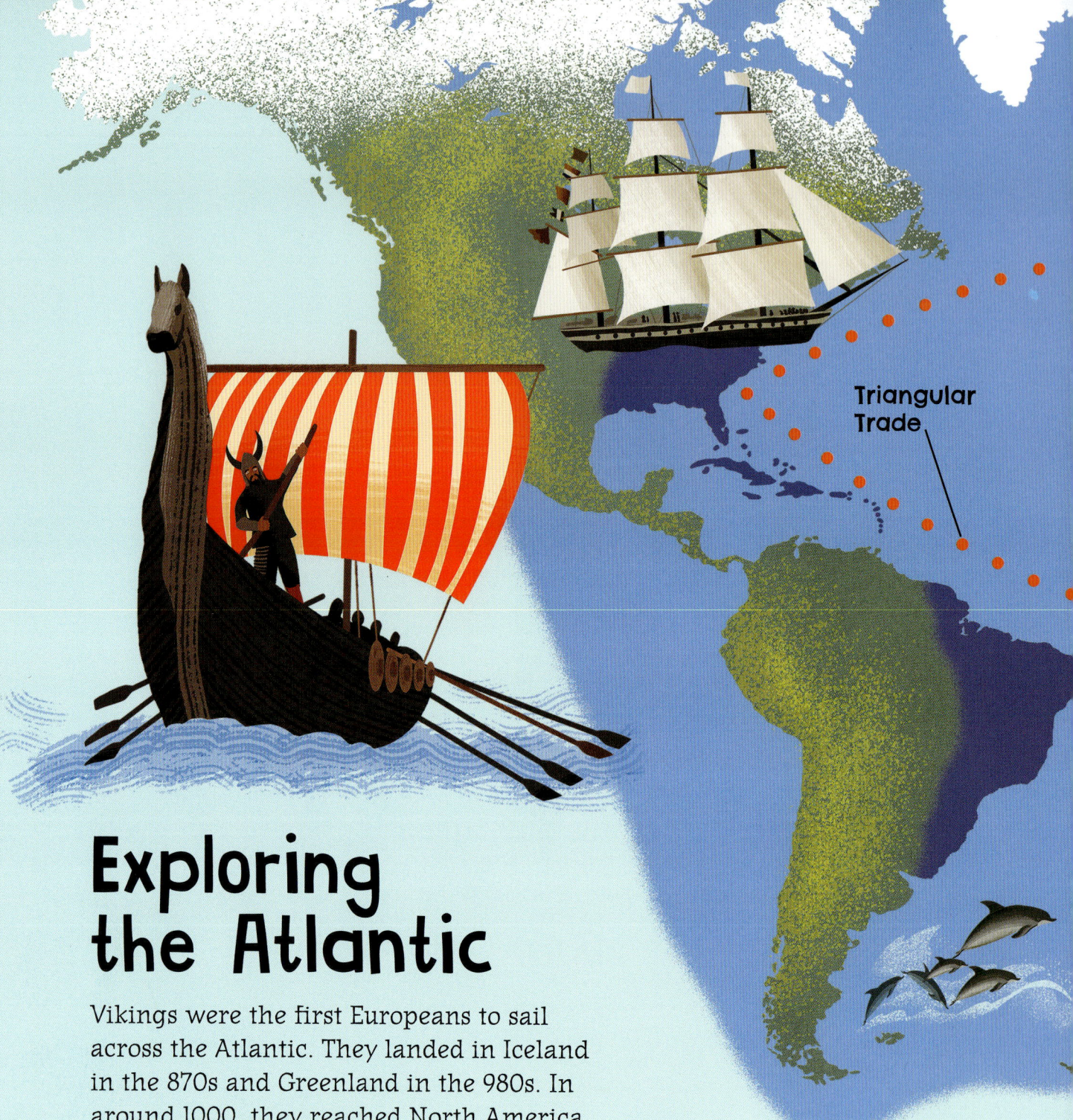

Triangular Trade

Exploring the Atlantic

Vikings were the first Europeans to sail across the Atlantic. They landed in Iceland in the 870s and Greenland in the 980s. In around 1000, they reached North America.

New contact

In 1492, Italian navigator Christopher Columbus set out across the Atlantic to discover new trade routes to Asia. Instead, he arrived in the Americas, which were already home to millions of indigenous peoples. This marked the beginning of the colonisation of the Americas by Europeans.

Trade and slavery

From the 1600s, Europeans transported people from Africa across the Atlantic to become slaves for settlers in the Americas. The crops grown by enslaved Africans were then shipped back to Europe to manufacture goods such as sugar and cotton cloth. These were sold to buy and enslave more African people. This was known as the Triangular Trade as it followed a roughly triangular route.

Undersea discoveries

The exploration of what lay under the Atlantic began in the 1870s, with an expedition by a British naval ship, HMS *Challenger*. Scientists on the *Challenger* confirmed the existence of the Mid-Atlantic Ridge. Further mapping of the ridge in the 1950s helped scientists to prove the theory of plate tectonics.

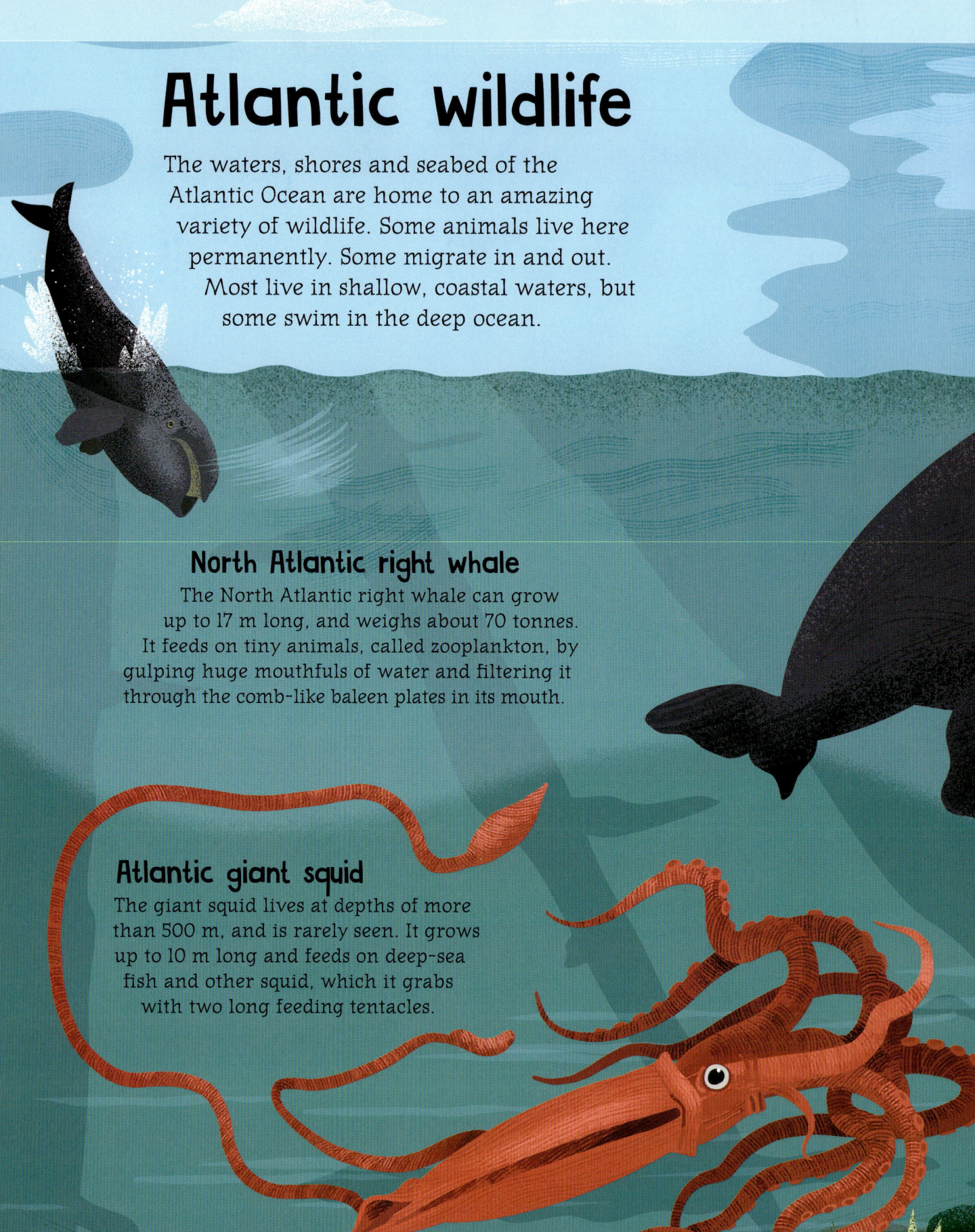

Atlantic wildlife

The waters, shores and seabed of the Atlantic Ocean are home to an amazing variety of wildlife. Some animals live here permanently. Some migrate in and out. Most live in shallow, coastal waters, but some swim in the deep ocean.

North Atlantic right whale
The North Atlantic right whale can grow up to 17 m long, and weighs about 70 tonnes. It feeds on tiny animals, called zooplankton, by gulping huge mouthfuls of water and filtering it through the comb-like baleen plates in its mouth.

Atlantic giant squid
The giant squid lives at depths of more than 500 m, and is rarely seen. It grows up to 10 m long and feeds on deep-sea fish and other squid, which it grabs with two long feeding tentacles.

Island cliffs

In the spring and summer, the rocky cliffs of the islands in the North Atlantic become home to millions of nesting seabirds. Gannets and other birds come to the cliffs to breed, spending the rest of the year out at sea.

In the depths

The Atlantic wolffish lives in deep, cold water. To stop its blood from freezing, the wolffish produces a chemical like antifreeze. A fearsome predator, it uses its strong jaws to feed on spiky sea urchins and sea snails.

The Sargasso Sea

At more than 3,000 km wide, the Sargasso Sea is a huge, calm haven in the middle of the Atlantic. With few currents, warm water and seaweed for shelter, it is the perfect spot for many ocean creatures to feed and rear their young.

Sargassum fish

Thanks to its colouring and ragged fins, the sargassum fish is perfectly hidden among the seaweed. This allows it to stalk its prey without being seen. The sargassum fish clambers through the seaweed, using its fins like arms. It darts forward to grab its prey – often fish as big as itself – sucking them into its large mouth.

Floating seaweed

The Sargasso Sea gets its name from a free-floating seaweed called sargassum. It is kept afloat by grape-like, air-filled bladders, and tangles together to form large mats on the sea's surface.

Sargassum crabs

While most crabs live on the seabed or the coast, the sargassum crab swims in the open ocean, weaving its way through strands of seaweed. The crab is camouflaged perfectly against the yellowish-brown colour of the sargassum, helping it to ambush its prey of fish and other crabs.

Eels

Each year, European eels make a journey of thousands of kilometres from rivers and lakes in Europe, across the Atlantic, to the Sargasso Sea to breed. The leaf-shaped eel larvae then drift on the ocean currents, maturing as they make their way back to Europe for their adult lives.

Atlantic green turtles

Some animals travel long distances through Atlantic waters in their lifetime, searching for food, or migrating to their breeding grounds. Among them are Atlantic green turtles.

Feeding and breeding
Green turtles spend most of their lives grazing on coastal seagrass. Every few years, they return to the beaches where they hatched so that they can breed. Some of these migrations are over 2,000 km long.

Laying eggs
At the beach, a female turtle digs a hole in the sand, above the high-tide line. Then she lays hundreds of eggs in her nest. After laying her eggs, she returns to the sea, and swims away.

Hatchlings

The eggs hatch around six to eight weeks later. The hatchlings usually emerge at night to avoid the heat of the Sun. As they make their way to the sea, many are eaten by gulls and crabs. Those who survive will one day travel back here to breed themselves.

People and transport

People have settled along almost every part of the Atlantic coastline, from icy Greenland to the tropical Caribbean islands. Ships criss-cross the ocean, carrying goods between major cities and ports.

Trade

The Atlantic is a vital shipping route between Europe, Africa and the Americas. Raw materials, such as iron ore, grain and coal, as well as finished goods, such as factory machinery and cars, are shipped between these continents. Cargo ships load and unload at huge ports, such as Rotterdam, Lagos, New York, and Rio de Janeiro.

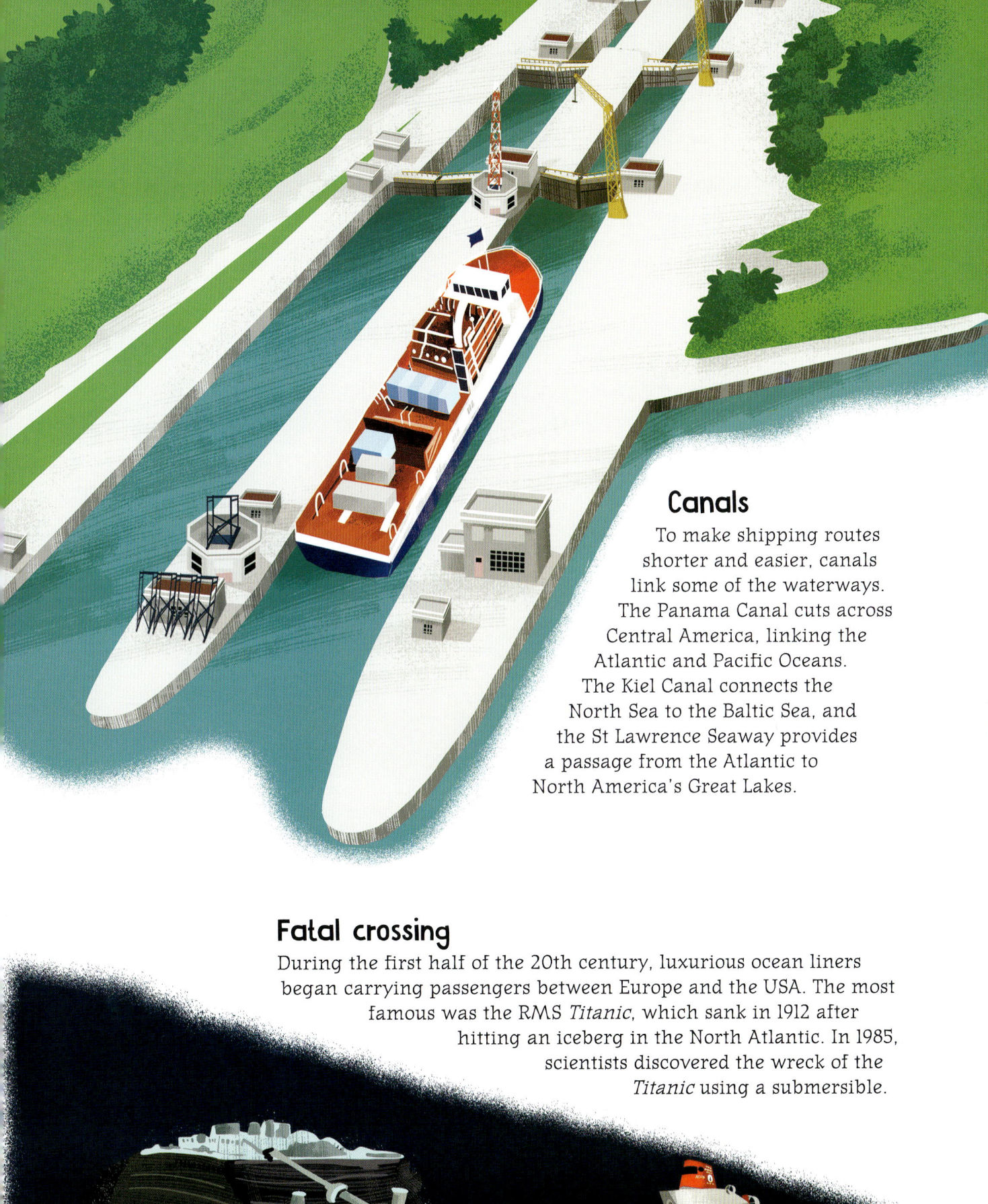

Canals

To make shipping routes shorter and easier, canals link some of the waterways. The Panama Canal cuts across Central America, linking the Atlantic and Pacific Oceans. The Kiel Canal connects the North Sea to the Baltic Sea, and the St Lawrence Seaway provides a passage from the Atlantic to North America's Great Lakes.

Fatal crossing

During the first half of the 20th century, luxurious ocean liners began carrying passengers between Europe and the USA. The most famous was the RMS *Titanic*, which sank in 1912 after hitting an iceberg in the North Atlantic. In 1985, scientists discovered the wreck of the *Titanic* using a submersible.

Riches of the Atlantic

The Atlantic provides us with a vast range of resources – food such as fish, crabs and lobsters, as well as oil and gas from under the ocean floor, precious stones and sea salt.

Drilling down

Oil and gas are fossil fuels, formed from the remains of animals and plants that lived millions of years ago. They are found trapped in rocks under the Atlantic seabed. Engineers drill down into the rocks from rigs to access them. People live and work on these rigs for weeks or months at a time to oversee the extraction.

Minerals

Minerals found in the Atlantic are vital raw materials for industries. Precious stones are found in some offshore sediments, such as diamonds off the coast of Namibia. Seawater itself is a valuable source of sea salt.

Natural beauty

Tourism is an important industry in the Atlantic, especially on the islands of the Caribbean, and the coasts of Europe and North America. Holidaymakers come to enjoy the beaches, water sports and activities, such as whale watching.

Fishing

Around a quarter of the total world catch of fish, crabs, shrimps and other marine animals comes from the waters of the Atlantic. More than 20 million tonnes are caught each year by commercial fishing fleets and local fishing boats.

Atlantic in danger

Like all the oceans, the Atlantic is being badly affected by human activities. These include catching too many fish, pouring and throwing waste into the water, and the effects of climate change.

Accidental danger

Atlantic creatures such as sharks and dolphins are often killed accidentally when they get caught up in fishing nets. Animals are also poisoned by pollution, trapped in old fishing nets, hit by ships and suffer stress from the noise of ship engines.

Overfishing

When too many of a species of fish are taken from the ocean, the fish cannot breed quickly enough to sustain numbers. This is called overfishing, and it disrupts the ocean's natural food chains. In the 1990s, the cod fishing industry of Newfoundland, Canada, completely collapsed due to overfishing. The cod population here still hasn't recovered.

Pollution

Enormous amounts of waste from the land end up in the Atlantic. Lots of floating waste, especially plastic, ends up in the Sargasso Sea, where it forms the North Atlantic Garbage Patch, measuring hundreds of kilometres across.

The future of the Atlantic

It is difficult for scientists to predict exactly what will happen to the Atlantic and its wildlife in the future. There are efforts to stop more harm by protecting animals, reducing pollution and cleaning up the damage already done. But there is a very long way to go.

Increasing temperatures
We are already seeing the effects of global warming in the Atlantic, where the sea temperature has increased by 0.58°C since the 1950s. Even such a small change has a huge effect on wildlife. For example, the number of lobsters living along the coast of North America has dropped, as the lobsters have moved to deeper, colder water.

Rising seas
Global warming is also causing glaciers and ice caps to melt, pouring more water into the oceans. The Atlantic sea level has already risen by about 15 cm since 1995. Without action to stop global warming, those levels might reach 2 m by the end of this century, which would be devastating for low-lying coastlines and their communities.

Cleaning up

In many countries, efforts are being made to reduce the amount of waste going into the Atlantic. Organisations such as Ocean Cleanup and Ocean Conservancy also plan to clean up the plastic rubbish already there.

Reversing the decline

Following the introduction of new fishing rules, some species are recovering after years of decline. Numbers of grey seals, and the white sharks that feed on them, declined in the 1980s and 1990s, but are now recovering well.

Atlantic facts

- The name Atlantic comes from 'Sea of Atlas' – the ancient Greek name for the waters beyond the Mediterranean Sea.

- In some places, the Atlantic is just a few hundred metres deep. In others, it plunges to more than 8 km. Its average depth is around 3,600 m.

- Plants can only survive in the top layer of the Atlantic Ocean. Light cannot penetrate below about 1,000 m, so it is too dark for plants to make food there.

- Each spring, as the Sun gets stronger after winter, there is an explosion in the amount of phytoplankton (plant plankton) in the North Atlantic. This is called the spring bloom.

- Rising cold currents, called upwellings, flow around western Africa and the Grand Banks of Newfoundland, bringing nutrients that help phytoplankton to thrive.

- The Atlantic Ocean varies greatly in width from west to east. It measures 2,850 km between Brazil and Africa, but 4,800 km between Florida, USA, and the Mediterranean.

- The area of the Atlantic Ocean is 82 million square km, without counting its surrounding seas. This is about the same as half of all the world's land.

- In winter and spring in the Northern Hemisphere, icebergs drift into the North Atlantic. These vast chunks of ice break off glaciers in Greenland, and melting sea ice in the Arctic.

- The Mid-Atlantic Ridge is the longest mountain range in the world, although it is mostly hidden under the sea.

- The world's tectonic plates move extremely slowly. The Atlantic is growing wider, but only at a rate of around 1 to 10 cm per year.

- At Thingvellir in Iceland, a narrow, rocky valley shows where the Mid-Atlantic Ridge crosses the island. For centuries, this was the site of Iceland's parliament, called the Althing.

- Tristan da Cunha is the Atlantic's most isolated inhabited island. Its closest neighbour is St Helena, some 2,120 km away.

- The British Isles are not volcanic islands, but are part of the European continent. They were cut off when sea levels rose thousands of years ago.

- In the days of sailing ships, seafarers crossed the Atlantic from Europe to the Americas using the easterly trade winds. They returned further north to take advantage of the westerlies.

- The waters of the North Atlantic are the saltiest of all the oceans. Much of the salt, dissolved in the water, flows out of the Mediterranean Sea.

Glossary

baleen hard plates in a baleen whale's mouth that act like a sieve to filter food out of seawater

camouflage a way of hiding by blending in with your surroundings

climate change gradual change of weather patterns, which includes global warming

colonisation taking control of an area that is home to other (indigenous) people

dissolve when a solid material becomes part of a liquid

food chain diagram that shows what animals eat; plants often start off a food chain

global warming increase in the Earth's temperature, caused by greenhouse gases

hemisphere half the Earth – the Northern Hemisphere stretches north of the equator, and the Southern Hemisphere stretches south of the equator

larva young of an animal, such as an insect, that will change shape before it becomes an adult (one larva; many larvae)

migration journey an animal makes either once in its lifetime or regularly, often to breed or feed

phytoplankton microscopic plants that drift in the ocean

sediment tiny pieces of solid material, such as grains of sand, that float in water or sink to the bottom of it

slavery when a person is owned by another and is made to work for them without being paid

strait narrow passage of water

subduction zone place where two tectonic plates are moving towards each other and one is pushed under the other

submersible vehicle for exploring underwater

sustain to keep something in its current state

tectonic plate section of the Earth's crust

water cycle never-ending process of water evaporating, forming clouds and falling back down to Earth in the form of rain or snow

zooplankton tiny, microscopic animals that float in the ocean and are often a source of food for larger animals, such as whales

Index

abyssal plain 9
African plate 9, 11
Ascension Island 7, 11
Azores 7, 11

baleen 16
Baltic Sea 7, 23
Bay of Fundy 4–5
breeding grounds 20

Canada 5, 27
cargo ships 22
Challenger [*see* HMS *Challenger*]
climate 12
climate change 26
colonisation 14
Columbus, Christopher 14
crabs 19, 21, 24–25
currents 4, 12–13, 18–19

dolphins 7, 26

eels 19
enslavement 15
Eurasian plate 8, 9, 11

fishing 25, 26–27, 29
fossil fuel 24

gannets 17
global warming 28
gravity 5
Gulf of Mexico 6, 13
Gulf Stream 13
gyres 13

hatchlings 21
HMS *Challenger* 15
hurricanes 12–13

icebergs 23
Iceland 7, 10, 14
island arc 11

Kiel Canal 23

larva (plural: larvae) 19
Lesser Antilles 6, 11
lobsters 24, 28

magma 9, 10–11
mapping 15
Mediterranean Sea 7
Mid-Atlantic Ridge 6–7, 9, 10, 11, 15
migrate 16, 20
Moon 5

North American plate 8–9
North Atlantic Garbage Patch 27

oil rigs 24
overfishing 27

Panama Canal 23
Pangaea 4
Panthalassa 4
polar 6
pollution 26–27, 28
port 22
predator 17
prey 18–19
Puerto Rico trench 8

RMS *Titanic* 23

Sargasso Sea 6, 18–19, 27
sargassum (seaweed) 19
sargassum crab 19
sargassum fish 18
scientists 15, 23, 28
seagrass 20
seagull 21
seals 7, 29

sea snails 17
sea urchins 17
sediment 6, 9, 24
sharks 26, 29
shipping route 22–23
South American plate 8–9
South Sandwich Islands 6–7, 11
squids (giant) 16
St Helena 7, 11
St Lawrence Seaway 23
Strait of Gibraltar 7
subduction zone 8, 11
submersible 23

tectonic plate 8–9, 15
thunderstorms 12–13
tides 4–5, 7, 20
Titanic [*see* RMS *Titanic*]
tourism 25
trade 14–15, 22
trade winds 12
transport 4, 15, 22–23
Triangular Trade (Atlantic) 15
Tristan da Cunha 7, 11
turtles 7, 20–21

Vikings 14
volcano 10–11

water cycle 4
weather 12–13
westerlies 12
whales 7, 16, 25
wind 12–13
wolffish 17